Matters of The Heart - The Reflective Journey Continues

1, Volume 1

S. M. Spencer

Published by S. M. Spencer, 2024.

MATTERS OF THE HEART - THE REFLECTIVE JOURNEY CONTINUES

First edition. October 22, 2024.

ISBN: 979-8227026620

Written by S. M. Spencer.

To my family and friends that have been here for me
during the hard times in my life.

THE MATTERS OF THE HEART
"The Reflective Journey Continues"
S. M. Spencer

In "MATTERS OF THE HEART: THE REFLECTIVE JOURNEY CONTINUES," I extend my heartfelt invitation to readers who joined me on a transformative odyssey.

Picking up where my earlier E-book "MATTERS OF THE HEART -THE REFLECTIVE JOURNEY" left off, I offer not just reflections but a roadmap to healing in the face of life's inevitable heartbreaks, rooted in my personal experiences, weaving together stories from my life that illustrate the complexities of love, loss, and recovery.

Through my poignant insights, I reflect on significant moments that have shaped my understanding of emotional resilience, lessons learned from my experiences and empowering individuals with practical strategies for moving forward.

I encourage readers to confront your fears and embrace vulnerability as a path to healing with hope, self-acceptance, and the transformative power of love, as you navigate their own challenges and the complexities of the human heart.

Matters of The Heart-The Reflective Journey Continues
Copyright@2024 by Shirley Spencer

TABLE OF CONTENTS

Chapter 1: The Journey Continues

The soft light of a late afternoon sun filtered through the sheer curtains of Ms. Spencer's cozy home office, casting a warm glow over the familiar surroundings. Nestled in her favorite office chair, Ms.

Spencer took a sip of her fragrant Earl Grey tea, savoring the comforting aroma as she allowed her gaze to wander over the cherished mementos that adorned the room.

Her eyes rested on the collection of framed photographs chronicled the joyful moments she had shared with her family over the years – laughter-filled gatherings, milestone celebrations, and quiet moments of connection. Shirley's lips curved into a gentle smile as she traced the faces of her loved ones, each image a thread in the tapestry of her life.

As she sank deeper into the cushion of the chair, Shirley felt a familiar sense of gratitude wash over her. The journey that had led her to this point had been one of both heartbreak and healing, and she knew that the lessons she had learned along the way had shaped her into the woman she was today.

Ms. Spencer's thoughts drifted back to her previous E-book, "Matters of the Heart: The Reflective Journey," where she had opened her heart to readers, sharing the intimate details of her experiences with love, loss, and self-discovery. That book had been a cathartic exploration, a way for her to process the complexities of the human heart and to find solace in the shared experiences of others.

Now, as she embarked on this new chapter, Ms. Spencer felt a renewed sense of purpose. She had witnessed firsthand the transformative power of vulnerability, the strength that could be found in the face of adversity. It was this wisdom that she now longed to impart to her readers, to guide them through the labyrinth of emotions that often accompanied the journey of the heart.

Ms. Spencer recalled a particularly poignant moment from her past, a time when she had mustered the courage to open herself up to another person, only to have her heart shattered by a painful breakup. In the aftermath, she had felt a deep sense of shame and vulnerability, unsure of how to move forward. But it was in that moment of darkness that she had discovered the true meaning of resilience.

"Resilience is not about being invincible," Shirley mused, her fingers tracing the rim of her teacup. "It's about bending, not breaking, in the face of adversity. Like a tree that sways in the wind, we must learn to adapt and grow, even in the midst of the storm."

As a life coach, Ms. Spencer's mission is to guide individuals through the complexities of heartbreak, helping them to cultivate the inner strength needed to navigate the winding path of healing.

"It's not an easy journey," she acknowledged, her gaze growing distant. "But it is one that is worth taking, for it is in the depths of our pain that we discover the true resilience of the human spirit."

Ms. Spencer's thoughts then turned to the support systems that had carried her through her own darkest moments. The comfort of her close-knit circle of friends, the unwavering love of her family – these were the pillars that had sustained her when she felt most alone.

She recalled a particular gathering, a time when her friends had rallied around her in the wake of a devastating loss. The warmth of their embrace, the gentle murmurs of understanding, and the shared tears had been a balm to her wounded heart. It was in those moments that Shirley had utterly understood the power of community, the way in which the shared experiences of others could provide a sense of belonging and healing.

"No one should have to navigate the complexities of the heart alone," Ms. Spencer said, her voice tinged with a quiet conviction. "We are all in this together, and it is by leaning on one another that we can find the strength to confront our fears and embrace the unknown."

As the sun dipped lower in the sky, casting a warm glow over the room, Ms. Spencer felt a renewed sense of purpose. This new journey, this "Matters of the Heart: The Reflective Journey Continues," was not just her own story – it was a tapestry woven with the experiences of individuals, each thread a testament to the resilience of the human spirit.

With a deep breath, she set down her teacup and turned her gaze to the window, her eyes shining with a spark of anticipation. "The journey continues," she murmured, "and I invite you, my dear readers, to join me once more as we explore the complexities of the heart, the depths of our pain, and the transformative power of love."

Chapter 2: The Very Essence That Makes Us Human

The warm afternoon sun filtered through the home office room windows of Ms. Shirley Spencer's cozy apartment, casting a gentle glow upon the well-worn office chair where she sat cradling a steaming cup of Earl Grey tea. The familiar scent of the fragrant brew mingled with the sweet aroma of blooming flower plant in her office area, creating a serene and inviting atmosphere.

With a serene smile, she drew parallels between the beauty of nature and the complexities of the human experience. "Just as these flowers require nurturing and care to thrive," she mused, "so too do the relationships and connections that give our lives meaning." Ms. Spencer's voice, rich with wisdom, carried a touch of wistfulness as she considered the delicate balance between the joys and challenges of being human.

Ms. Spencer allowed her gaze to drift to the framed photograph on the mantelpiece – a cherished memory of her dearest friend, whose sudden passing had left an indelible mark on her soul. "It was during one of the darkest periods of my life that I truly learned the power of reflection," she said, her eyes reflecting the weight of that experience. "When I lost my dear friend, the grief threatened to consume me. But in the stillness of my office, much like this one, I found solace in revisiting our memories, honoring the beauty of our friendship, and allowing myself to fully feel the sorrow that accompanied her absence."

As she spoke, Ms. Spencer's voice grew softer, tinged with the bittersweet notes of a life well-lived. "Reflection is not merely an act of looking back," she continued, "but a profound acknowledgment of the impact others has had on our lives. It is in these moments of introspection that we uncover the true resilience that lies within us the strength to weather the storms and emerge with a deeper understanding of ourselves and the world around us."

Reaching for her journal, Ms. Spencer opened its well-worn pages and began to flip through the entries, her fingers tracing the lines of her own handwriting. "I encourage each of you to engage in your own reflective practices," she said, her gaze meeting that of her unseen audience. "Whether it be through journaling, meditation, or simply quiet contemplation, allow yourself to explore the depths of your experiences, both joyful and sorrowful. For it is in this process of self-discovery that we find the courage to face the challenges that lie ahead."

The chapter continued as Ms. Spencer shared a poignant story from her early career, a time when she had faced a significant professional setback that threatened to undermine her confidence. As she recounted the memory, her voice wavered with vulnerability, but she quickly steadied it, her eyes shining with a newfound resolve.

"In that moment, I felt the weight of self-doubt pressing down upon me," she admitted, "but I soon realized that resilience is not about avoiding pain, but rather about embracing it, learning from it, and emerging stronger than before." Ms. Spencer paused, her gaze drifting to the window, where the sunlight danced across her window. "Resilience is a skill that can be cultivated, nurtured, and honed over time. It is the very essence that allows us to weather the storms of life and find the strength to continue our journey."

As the chapter unfolded, Ms. Spencer's reflections delved deeper, exploring the societal context of aging and emotional well-being. She shared her observations about the stigma surrounding vulnerability in older adults, shedding light on the need for open conversations about grief, love, and loss.

"Too often, we are told that as we grow older, we must simply 'accept' the challenges we face, as if our emotions are somehow less valid or worthy of attention," she said, her brow furrowing with concern. "But the truth is, the heart knows no age. Our capacity for love, for sorrow, and for growth is timeless. It is our responsibility, as a society, to create a space where individuals of all ages can embrace their emotions without shame or judgment."

Pausing to take a sip of her tea, Ms. Spencer's gaze grew distant, as if she were reliving the experience. "Those formative moments," she continued, "they shape our understanding of compassion and the bonds we forge with others. They teach us that true connection is born not from perfection, but from the willingness to be vulnerable and to share in each other's struggles."

The chapter then shifted to a more introspective tone as Ms. Spencer reflected on the challenges that come with being human. "Heartbreak," she said, her voice tinged with a hint of melancholy, "is a universal experience, one that can leave us feeling isolated and alone." She recounted a poignant moment from her own early adulthood, when the end of a significant romantic relationship had left her world dimmed and her heart shattered.

"In that moment, the pain felt all-consuming, as if the very ground beneath me had crumbled." Ms. Spencer's words were laced with empathy, her eyes shining with the memory of that anguish. "Yet, it was in the embrace of my friends and family that I found the strength to move forward. They rallied around me, providing a support system that illuminated my path back to hope."

Leaning forward, Ms. Spencer's expression grew more animated as she introduced the concept of emotional intelligence. "You see, my dear readers, understanding and managing our emotions is the very essence that makes us human. It is the foundation upon which we build our connections with others."

With the wisdom of her professional years, Ms. Spencer shared insights from her work, illustrating the transformative power of emotional awareness. "I remember a client who struggled to articulate their feelings, trapped in a cycle of misunderstandings and resentment. But through self-reflection and practice, they learned to express themselves authentically, leading to healthier relationships and a greater sense of self-acceptance."

Her voice was both nurturing and empowering as she encouraged readers to explore their own emotional landscapes. "When we embrace our emotions, when we learn to navigate the complexities of our inner worlds, we unlock the true potential of our connections with others. It is a dance, where two individuals must learn to move together, sometimes stumbling, but always striving for harmony."

With a gentle smile, she concluded, "My dear readers, I invite you to embrace your relationships with open hearts. For it is in the journey of understanding one another, in all its complexities, that we find the true beauty of the human experience. Let us move forward, hand in hand, nurturing the connections that enrich our lives and shape the very essence of who we are."

Chapter 3: The Transformative Power of Love

It is Saturday night I am sitting in my home office listening to a jazz song "Awakening", thinking about one of the coldest raw aspects of life, "The Matters of The Heart".

Tomorrow is valentine's day, one of a female's precious day in her life. A day I have not had the pleasure to experience. I am talking about a real romantic experience of a lifetime; you only dream about.

The handsome man that sweeps me off my feet was no longer a part of my life. I remember speaking to him on a Thursday night, our conversation was the beginning of the end, the 28th of January 2021. We spoke again on Sunday January 31,2021 and I knew then that it was all over. The next day February 1, 2021, I texted him to confirm it was over and wow, he had me blocked.

Although I was a bit surprised, he blocked my number, I was somewhat relieved. He did for me what I did not have the courage to do myself. What I could not understand was how this man could continuous expressed how he loved and cared for me but could just walk away without a word.

I wonder if any of the expressions of his love and his encouraging words were for real or just talk and game. It is ok to wake up one morning and not love someone anymore, it is ok to want to have just a sexual relationship with someone, but it not ok to discard the matters of a person's heart, for the heart is connected to a person's soul. All the things a person can do to a person, the matters of the heart are a cold raw deal that could destroy an individual's well-being and turn their world upside down which can and will alter their future.

That day he blocked my number, Although I felt a spiritually release and the bond broke in a split moment, "I felt as though a part of me had been ripped away, leaving a gaping hole that could never be filled." Yet, even in the depths of her grief, Shirley had found solace in the love that had sustained her throughout her life.

The unwavering support of her family and close-knit circle of friends had been a lifeline, a reminder that she was not alone in her journey of healing. "It was their love, their compassion, which carried me through the darkest of days," Shirley said, her eyes glistening with unshed tears. "They surrounded me with their embrace, their words of comfort, a testament to the enduring power of familial love."

"I have learned the importance of family, of cherishing the bonds that connect us," Shirley reflected. Love is not just a feeling, but a commitment – to support one another, to celebrate each other's triumphs, and to mourn each other's losses." Shirley felt a deep sense of gratitude for the love that had shaped her life. She thought of the countless hours she had spent with family members, the inside jokes they shared, and the unwavering support they had provided throughout the years.

"Familial love is the foundation upon which we build our lives," Shirley said, her voice filled with conviction. "It is the safe haven where we can be our true selves, where we can find solace in times of need and rejoice in moments of joy." Shirley's thoughts then drifted to the friendships that had enriched her journey, the deep connections that had provided a sense of belonging and understanding. She recalled a particularly poignant moment, when a dear friend had stood by her side during the darkest days of her grief.

It was in those moments of vulnerability that Shirley had discovered the true power of platonic love – the way it could provide a sense of safety, acceptance, and mutual understanding. "Friendship is a sacred bond, one that transcends the boundaries of romantic

love," Shirley said, her gaze distant yet resolute. "It is a connection forged through shared experiences, laughter, and the willingness to be there for one another, no matter what life may bring."

Ms. Spencer contemplated the various forms of love that had graced her life. From the all-encompassing embrace of familial love to the deep, abiding connections of friendship, each had played a vital role in shaping her journey. "And then, there is the love that sets our hearts aflame," Shirley murmured, her eyes softening as she gazed at the photograph of her and Jack. "The kind that ignites a spark within us, that makes the world seem brighter and more vibrant."

"But love, in all its forms, is not without its challenges," Shirley acknowledged, her brow furrowing slightly. "For with the joy and connection it brings, there also comes the potential for heartbreak and loss." In this life we as people have to go through some things in our lifetime to experience some things before, we can feel somethings in order to understand some things.

"My dear readers, I invite you to embrace the transformative power of love," Ms. Spencer said, her voice filled with a quiet conviction. "Whether it be the love of family, the deep bonds of friendship, or the all-consuming passion of a romantic partnership, let it be the guiding light that illuminates your path, even in the darkest of times. "For it is in the depths of our hearts that we find the strength to overcome any challenge, to heal from any heartbreak, and to live life to the fullest."

Chapter 4: The Complexities of Intimate Relationships

The soft rays of the afternoon sun filtered through the sheer curtains, casting a warm glow over the familiar surroundings of Ms. Spencer's cozy study. Seated at her writing desk, Shirley's fingers traced the delicate edges of the letters and mementos that adorned the surface, each one a thread in the tapestry of her life's intimate connections.

Her gaze settled on a faded photograph; the edges worn from years of gentle handling. In the image, a young woman with sparkling eyes and a radiant smile stood beside a handsome man, their arms entwined as they gazed into each other's eyes. Ms. Spencer's lips curved into a wistful smile as she remembered that moment, the fluttering heartbeats and the sweet anticipation of their serious romance.

"It was like something out of a storybook," Ms. Spencer murmured, her fingers caressing the worn edges of the photograph. "The way our eyes met across the crowded room, the electricity that seemed to crackle between us – it was enough to make my heart race with excitement and nerves."

She recalled the tentative first steps of their relationship, the stolen glances and the shy, fleeting touches that had ignited a fire within her. She could almost feel the warmth of his hand in hers, the way their fingers had intertwined as they explored the world together, discovering the depths of their connection with each passing day.

"Those early days were filled with such a sense of wonder and possibility," Ms. Spencer said, her voice tinged with nostalgia.

"We were young, naive, and utterly captivated by the magic of falling in love."

Yet, as with any relationship, the path was not always smooth. Ms. Spencer's gaze grew distant as she remembered the challenges they had faced, the moments when communication had broken down and misunderstandings had threatened to tear them apart.

"There were times when we just couldn't seem to see eye to eye," she admitted, her brow furrowing slightly. "We'd argue, voices raised, both of us feeling misunderstood and isolated, until the tension became almost unbearable."

She recalled one particularly painful argument, the memory of it still etched in her mind. She had felt her heart racing, the words tumbling out in a desperate attempt to make her partner understand. But the more she tried to explain herself, the more the distance between them seemed to grow.

"I can still feel the ache in my chest, the way my throat tightened with unshed tears," she said, her voice barely above a whisper. "In that moment, I felt so alone, so disconnected from the person I loved the most."

Ms. Spencer took a deep, steadying breath, her fingers tracing the worn edges of the photograph once more. "It was a turning point for us, a moment that forced us to confront the cracks in our relationship and the importance of open communication and vulnerability."

Lifting her gaze, Ms. Spencer's eyes shone with a newfound resolve. "Intimate relationships are not without their challenges, my dear readers. They require us to be willing to open our hearts, to share our fears and our dreams, and to navigate the complexities of human connection."

Ms. Spencer's thoughts then drifted to a recent wedding she had attended, the joyous celebration a stark contrast to the bittersweet memories of her own marriage. She recalled the laughter that had filled the air, the heartfelt toasts, and the way the newlyweds had gazed at each other with such raw, unabashed love.

"As I watched them exchange their vows, I couldn't help but feel a twinge of nostalgia," she admitted, her voice tinged with a hint of wistfulness. "The way their eyes shone with pure adoration, the way their hands trembled as they held each other – it was a reminder of the exhilaration and the vulnerability that come with falling in love."

She paused, her gaze drifting to the window, where the vibrant sunlight and tree branches swayed gently in the breeze. "Love is a complex and ever-evolving force, my dear readers. It can lift us to the heights of joy and plunge us into the depths of sorrow, often in the span of a single heartbeat."

With a deep breath, she turned her attention back to the photograph, her fingers tracing the outline of her late husband's face. "My own journey with love has been a winding path, filled with both triumph and heartbreak. But it is through these experiences that I have come to understand the true value of vulnerability and the importance of establishing healthy boundaries within our intimate relationships."

Ms. Spencer recalled a time when she had struggled to assert her own needs, often prioritizing her partner's desires over her own. "I was so afraid of rocking the boat, of causing conflict or disrupting the delicate balance of our relationship," she admitted, her brow furrowing slightly. "But in doing so, I slowly began to lose touch with my authentic self, compromising my own happiness and well-being.

" It wasn't until I decided to speak up, to communicate my boundaries and my needs, that I experienced a profound shift in my perspective. "I realized that true intimacy is not about suppressing our own desires, but about finding the courage to share them – to be vulnerable and to trust that our partner will meet us halfway."

Ms. Spencer's eyes sparkled with a newfound determination as she shared the strategies, she had learned for establishing healthy boundaries within her relationships. "It's about being clear and direct in our communication, about setting limits and respecting the needs of both individuals," she explained, her voice firm yet compassionate.

"And it's not just about our romantic partnerships, my dear readers," she added, her gaze sweeping across the room. "These principles apply to all of our intimate connections, whether it be with family, friends, or even our professional relationships."

"Intimate relationships are the very fabric of our lives, woven together by the threads of love, trust, and understanding," she said, her voice soft but resolute. "And it is our responsibility to nurture and protect these connections, to ensure that they grow and flourish in a way that honors the needs of all involved."

"I invite you, my dear readers, to embark on this exploration of the complexities of intimate relationships," she said, her lips curving into a gentle smile. "To confront your fears, to communicate your needs, and to embrace the transformative power of vulnerability for it is in the depths of our connections that we find the truest reflection of ourselves." "The journey continues," she murmured.

Chapter 5: Navigating Grief and Loss

The soft patter of raindrops against the
windowpane created a soothing rhythm that enveloped Ms.
Spencer's home office, as if the heavens themselves were weeping
in sympathy. Nestled in her favorite office chair, she cradled a
steaming mug of Earl Grey tea, it's comforting aroma mingling
with the earthy scent of the rain outside.

Ms. Spencer's gaze was fixed on the dancing droplets, her
mind drifting back to a time when the anguish of grief had
threatened to consume her. The memory played out vividly in
her mind, a painful recollection that she knew she must confront
if she were to guide her readers through the complexities of the
human heart.

"It was a call that shattered my world," she murmured, her
fingers tightening around the delicate porcelain of her mug. "The
kind that leaves you frozen, unable to comprehend the words
being spoken."

She recalled the moment; the phone rang the nurse from
the hospital to come quick. In that instant, the floor seemed to
vanish beneath her feet, and she felt as though she were falling,
spiraling into a void of raw, unbridled sorrow.

"The pain was physical, a weight that pressed against my
chest, making it difficult to breathe," it was as if my very soul was
weeping." She recalls rushing into the hospital room where her
mother was lying as if she was asleep. She closed her eyes as she
felt a range of complex emotions. It was if there was a sudden
destruction of the world I use to know. I felt she was taken away
without any warning.

Later that afternoon, she reconstructs events in her mind, looking back at the time leading up to her mother's death and

searching for clues that could have indicated what was to come.

As time passed on, she recalled how she had immersed herself in the mundane tasks of daily life, a desperate attempt to maintain a sense of normalcy in the face of overwhelming loss. "I kept myself busy, busier than I had been in years, as if the sheer force of my will would somehow will away the reality of her absence."

As she recounted each stage of her grief, she drew upon her professional expertise as a former mental health counselor, offering insights into the complex and often nonlinear nature of the grieving process. "It's important to understand that grief is not a linear journey," she mphasized. "We may find ourselves cycling back and forth between the stages, revisiting emotions we thought we had overcome."

I recall, it was my mother's birthday, the tears rolling down my face, unstoppable, a friend called and reminded me of the gift I was left with. The night before my mother's death I was given the unforgettable opportunity to spend the last hours of her life alive with her. I suddenly comprehended the events that night revealed she was preparing me for the dramatically change to come.

Her thoughts then turned to the day of her mother's funeral, a moment that had both shattered and strengthened her. She described the somber atmosphere, the air thick with the weight of shared sorrow, as family and friends gathered to honor the life of the woman they had loved.

She recalled, her eyes glistening with unshed tears. "But as I spoke of the memories we had shared, the laughter we had cherished, I felt a profound sense of connection – not just with my mother, but with all those who had gathered to mourn her."

"I realized that the act of sharing our stories, of honoring the lives of those we have lost, is a powerful testament to the enduring bonds of love and community."

She described the collective outpouring of emotion that had swept through the crowd, the tears and laughter mingling as they celebrated the vibrant spirit of her mother. "It was a reminder that we are not alone in our grief, that the pain we feel is a shared experience that can bring us closer together."

Ms. Spencer's gaze then shifted to the window, where the rain had begun to slow, the droplets clinging to the glass like delicate tears. "In the aftermath of loss, it's so easy to become consumed by guilt, to feel as though we are betraying the memory of our loved ones by finding moments of joy," she said, her voice tinged with a hint of self-reflection.

"But I've come to learn that self-compassion is essential in the grieving process. To honor the memory of those we've lost, we must also honor the beauty of life, the fleeting moments of happiness that they would have wanted us to cherish."

"It's a lesson I had to learn, but one that has transformed my understanding of grief and the resilience of the human spirit."

"Grief is not a linear journey, my dear readers," she said, her voice soft but resolute. "It is a winding path that tests the limits of our strength, but it is also a testament to the power of the human heart to heal and grow."

The exploration of the grief process is a newfound determination to embrace the full spectrum of emotions that come with loss, and to discover the transformative power of self-compassion and shared connection.

Chapter 6 - The Road Map to Healing

The warm glow of the desk lamp cast a soft light over Ms. Spencer's cozy study, illuminating the collection of journals and books on emotional healing that surrounded her. As she sipped her fragrant Earl Grey tea, her gaze drifted from the pages of her latest notes to the rain-streaked window, where the evening shadows were beginning to settle. With a pensive sigh, she leaned back in her chair, her fingers tracing the worn leather cover of her journal.

"The journey of the heart is never a straight path," she murmured, her voice tinged with the wisdom of experience. "It winds and turns, testing our resilience at every step." Ms. Spencer knew this truth intimately, having navigated the ups and downs of her own healing journey. Now, as she prepared to share her insights with her readers, she was determined to offer a roadmap that would empower others to embrace their own unique paths to recovery.

Closing her eyes, Ms. Spencer allowed her mind to drift back to a pivotal moment in her life, when a profound heartbreak had threatened to shatter her very foundation. The end of a long-term relationship had left her reeling, the shock and sadness washing over her in relentless waves. "I felt so lost, so adrift," she recalled, her brow furrowing at the memory. "The future I had envisioned had crumbled, and I had no idea how to pick up the pieces."

In the days and weeks that followed, Ms. Spencer had found solace in the simple act of putting pen to paper, pouring out her thoughts and emotions onto the pages of her journal. The cathartic release of writing had been a lifeline, allowing her to acknowledge the depth of her pain and begin the process of acceptance. "It wasn't easy," she admitted, "but with each word I wrote, I could feel a weightlifting from my shoulders."

Gradually, Ms. Spencer had begun to incorporate other self-care practices into her daily routine, finding solace in the rhythmic motions of the soothing melodies of her favorite music. "I realized that healing wasn't just about moving on," she explained, her eyes shining with understanding. "It was about integrating the past into a new narrative of strength and resilience."

With a gentle smile, Ms. Spencer opened her journal and began to outline the steps of her "Healing Plan," a structured approach that she had developed through her own experiences and her work as a professional life coach. "The first step is to set your intentions," she said, her pen gliding across the page. "What do you hope to achieve through this journey? What do you need to heal?"

As she spoke, Ms. Spencer shared examples from her own life, recounting how she had set specific goals for herself, such as reconnecting with her passions and rebuilding her support network. "It's important to be honest with yourself," she emphasized, "to really delve into the root causes of your pain and what you need to address."

The next component of the plan, she explained, was to identify emotional triggers – those moments or situations that threatened to unravel the progress she had made. "I found that keeping a journal was incredibly helpful in this regard," Ms. Spencer revealed. "By tracking my thoughts and feelings, I was able to recognize patterns and develop strategies to manage my reactions."

One such strategy, she recalled, had been the discovery of growing plants and listening to music as a therapeutic outlet. "There was something about the rhythmic motions of tending to my plants, the way the earth seemed to ground me," she said, her eyes sparkling with recollection. "It became a sacred space where I could process my emotions and find a sense of peace."

Ms. Spencer's voice softened as she spoke of the importance of community and support in the healing process. She shared a poignant story of a support group she had attended during her own journey, where individuals had gathered to share their experiences and offer one another encouragement. "The sense of camaraderie and understanding in that room was palpable," she recalled. "It was a safe space where we could be vulnerable, where we could lean on each other and know that we were not alone."

Reaching across the desk, Ms. Spencer gently placed her hand on the journal, her gaze warm and inviting. "Healing is not a solitary endeavor," she said, her tone laced with compassion. "Reach out to your loved ones, your support network. Allow yourself to be seen and heard, to draw strength from the connections that sustain you."

As the chapter drew to a close, Ms. Spencer's expression took on a contemplative cast. "The journey of healing is not linear," she acknowledged, "but rather a winding river, with currents that ebb and flow." She paused, her eyes reflecting the metaphorical waters she described. "But it is in navigating those currents, in embracing the challenges and the beauty that emerges, that we find our true resilience."

With a renewed sense of purpose, Ms. Spencer closed her journal and turned her gaze to the rain-streaked window, where the last vestiges of daylight were fading.

"So, my dear readers," she said, her voice carrying a note of encouragement, "I invite you to embark on your own healing journey. Reflect on your experiences, take actionable steps, and know that the path ahead, though winding, is one of transformation and growth." She smiled, the light in her eyes igniting a spark of hope. "The future may seem uncertain, but with open hearts and resilient spirits, we can navigate it together."

Chapter 7: Embracing Vulnerability

The warm glow of the afternoon sun casts a gentle light across the familiar surroundings, lending an air of serenity.

Embracing vulnerability does not come easy. Opening your heart and sharing your true feelings, letting your guard down and revealing your innermost thoughts and emotions can fill you with a sense of dread." Yet, vulnerability is not a weakness, but a strength. It takes immense courage to open yourself up, to allow others to see the depths of your heart."

Ultimately, it is not easy because you open yourself up to the possibility of emotional attack, being hurt and potential criticism or rejection. The risk is worth it, not trying to avoid emotional pain is limiting yourself from the desires and possibility of accepting and experiencing a romantic relationship. Embracing vulnerability can lead to personal growth, self-discovery and emotional strength.

The true strength lies not in the mask of invulnerability, but in the willingness to be authentic, to embrace the full spectrum of our emotions," "It is a lesson that will shape the rest of your journey, both personally and professionally." Confronting your fears and opening up to the possibility of growth and healing is a transformative power of vulnerability.

The societal perceptions of vulnerability are not always so kind. Some people embrace the idea, acknowledging the strength it takes to be vulnerable," But others may cling to the notion that vulnerability is a sign of weakness, something to be avoided at all costs.

It's a perception that is all too common, especially among older adults. They are expected to maintain a facade of stoicism, to present an image of unwavering strength and resilience. But in doing so, often deny themselves the very thing that can help them heal and grow."

Ms. Spencer gazed upon the framed photographs that adorned the mantel, each one a testament to the power of connection and the beauty that can arise from vulnerability. She remembered the grief that had threatened to consume her when she had lost several of her beloved family members, the heaviness in her heart that had threatened to overwhelm her.

"In the depths of my sorrow, I found myself isolated, unable to share the full weight of my emotions," Ms. Spencer said, her voice tinged with a hint of pain. "But it was when I finally allowed myself to be vulnerable, to open up to my loved ones, that the healing process began."

She recalled the warmth of their embrace, the gentle murmurs of understanding, and the shared tears that had forged an unbreakable bond. "It was in that moment that I realized the true strength that can be found in vulnerability. By allowing myself to be seen, to be heard, I found the support and connection I so desperately needed."

"I've since made it my mission to help others understand the transformative power of vulnerability. To create safe spaces where people can share their stories, their fears, and their triumphs without judgment."

She remembered a coaching group she had led, where participants had hesitantly shared their personal experiences, the air thick with a mixture of anxiety and anticipation. "As the session progressed, I watched the walls come down, the masks fall away. In their place, a profound sense of trust and connection blossomed, forged through the shared vulnerability of those in the zoom room."

Ms. Spencer smiled, her heart swelling with a deep sense of purpose. "It's in those moments that I see the true strength of the human spirit. When we have the courage to be vulnerable, to show our authentic selves, we unlock a wellspring of resilience and understanding that can carry us through even the darkest of times."

"The journey of embracing vulnerability is a journey worth taking, for it is in the depths of our fears that we find the courage to truly live."

To embrace the transformative power of vulnerability and the exploration of the heart is the openness of our souls to truly connect, heal, and grow. The journey continues.

Chapter 8 - The Power of Forgiveness

With a pensive gaze, Ms. Spencer leaned back in her chair, her mind drifting to a time when the weight of resentment and anger had threatened to consume her. The memory of that painful betrayal by a close friend still lingered, a shadow that had once darkened her days and restless nights. She recalled the sleepless hours spent ruminating over the past, the emotions of hurt and disappointment churning within her, taking a toll on her mental well-being.

"Forgiveness," she murmured, the word rolling off her tongue with a mixture of reverence and resolve. It was a concept she had grappled with, a journey she had navigated with both trepidation and determination. As she sat in the comfort of her home, Ms. Spencer knew that acknowledging those raw feelings had been the first step toward healing.

Closing her eyes, she allowed the vivid

recollection to unfold. The day she had finally confronted her friend, the source of her pain, the air in the room had felt thick with unspoken words and emotions. With a racing heart, Ms. Spencer had mustered the courage to express her hurt and disappointment, her voice wavering at first, then growing steadier as the words poured out.

The tension in the room had been palpable, but as they both opened-up, a shared history emerged, one that had been obscured by the fog of resentment. In that moment of vulnerability, Ms. Spencer realized that forgiveness was not about condoning the wrongs done, but about reclaiming her own peace of mind. It was a transformative act, a means of freeing herself from the shackles of anger and resentment.

With a deep breath, Ms. Spencer's thoughts shifted to the concept of self-forgiveness, a theme that held a special place in her heart. She recalled a time when she had felt she had failed herself in a professional setting, the feelings of inadequacy and guilt weighing heavily on her. These emotions had led her to question her own worth, impacting her relationships and overall happiness.

Through a series of reflective exercises, such as journaling and meditation, Ms. Spencer had gradually learned to forgive herself for her perceived shortcomings. She understood that self-forgiveness was an essential step in the healing journey, a means of liberating oneself from the shackles of guilt and embracing growth.

As she reflected on the broader implications of forgiveness in her life, Ms. Spencer's mind drifted to her relationships with family members. She recalled a particular incident with one of her adult children, where misunderstandings had created a distance between them. With warmth and honesty, she described the heart-to-heart conversation that followed, where both had expressed their grievances and listened to each other's perspectives.

This dialogue had become a turning point, allowing them to rebuild trust and strengthen their bond. Ms. Spencer emphasized how this experience had reinforced her belief that forgiveness was a two- way street, requiring openness and understanding from all parties involved. It was a journey that demanded vulnerability, but one that ultimately led to profound emotional freedom and deeper connections.

With a heart full of wisdom, Ms. Spencer knew that forgiveness was not a one-time act, but a continuous journey. She invited readers to reflect on their own experiences, to approach the process with compassion and understanding. "Forgiveness," she whispered, "is the key that unlocks the door to emotional freedom and deeper connections. It is a gift we can give ourselves, and in turn, share with those we hold dear."

Conflict in inmate relationships will take a toll on the well-being of the relationship. Happiness depends on how you recover from difficult and hurtful experiences. Marital satisfaction fosters in the ability to forgive and seek forgiveness.

Studies reported that partners who were committed to cooperation tend to become competitive after betrayal and start keeping scores in arguments versus seeking compromise and enjoyment of each other's company (Hall & Fincham, 2005).

Relationship researcher John Gottman also found that blame and defensiveness tend to contribute to the deterioration of relationships over time (Gottman & Silver, 2015).

As the gentle breeze rustled the leaves, Ms. Spencer felt a renewed sense of purpose. She knew that by sharing her own story, she could inspire others to embark on their own transformative journeys, to let go of the burdens that had weighed them down and embrace the power of forgiveness.

Chapter 9: The Balance, Self-Protection and Desire

The warm rays of the afternoon sun streamed through the kitchen window, casting a gentle glow over Ms. Spencer's familiar surroundings. With steaming mug of Earl Grey tea cradled in her hands, her gaze drifted to the trees outside of her kitchen window.

Ms. Spencer's mind drifted back to a time when the balance between self-protection and the desire for connection had not come so easily to her. She recalled a particular social gathering, years ago, where she had felt an instant spark of recognition with a fellow attendee – a connection that had both thrilled and terrified her. "My heart was racing, the anticipation building with each passing moment," She murmured, her fingers tracing the rim of her teacup. "But the moment I felt that initial pull towards him, my mind was flooded with memories of past heartbreaks, and I found myself retreating into the safety of my own shell."

She remembered the way she had subtly distanced herself, her polite smiles and casual conversation masking the turmoil within. "I was so afraid of being vulnerable, of opening myself up to the possibility of rejection or pain," she admitted, her brow furrowing slightly. "And so, I built walls, convinced that if I kept my distance, I could somehow protect myself from the anguish of another broken heart."

Ms. Spencer gaze drifted to the framed photograph on the mantel, a candid shot of her and her ex-husband, their arms wrapped around each other, laughter etched upon their faces. The memory of his warm embrace and infectious chuckle washed over her, a bittersweet reminder of the profound connection they had shared.

"With him, it was different," she said, a wistful smile playing on her lips. "The moment our eyes met across the crowded room; I felt a spark of electricity that I had never experienced before. And despite the fears that threatened to consume me, I found the courage to take that leap of faith, to open my heart to the possibility of love."

She recalled the exhilaration of their first date, the way her heart had fluttered with each fleeting touch and shared laugh. "It was as if the world around us had faded away, and all that mattered was the connection we were forging, the bond that was blossoming between us."

Yet, even in the depths of their love, Ms. Spencer had struggled to find the balance between self-protection and the desire for intimacy. "There were times when I would catch myself holding back,

afraid to fully commit, to let down my guard and reveal the depths of my feelings," she confessed, her voice tinged with a hint of regret.

Her thoughts then drifted to a recent conversation she had had with one of her coaching clients, a young woman who had been grappling with a similar dilemma.

"She came to me, her eyes brimming with a mixture of excitement and trepidation," Ms. Spencer recalled, her expression softening. "She had met someone, she told me, and she felt a connection she had never experienced before. But the fear of getting hurt, of losing that sense of control, was holding her back."

Ms. Spencer had listened intently, drawing upon her own experiences to offer guidance and support. "I shared with her the lessons I had learned, the importance of recognizing our emotional boundaries and communicating them effectively," she explained, her voice calm and measured.

"It's not about building impenetrable walls, my dear," Ms. Spencer had said to her client, her gaze warm and reassuring. "It's about finding the courage to open our hearts, while still maintaining a sense of self-protection – to strike that delicate balance between vulnerability and self-care."

She recalled the way her client's eyes had widened with understanding, the weight of her words sinking in. "She realized that true intimacy is not about sacrificing our own needs, but about finding the strength to share them – to trust that the person we've chosen to connect with will meet us halfway, respecting our boundaries and honoring our desires."

Ms. Spencer contemplated the lessons she had learned over the years. "It's a balance that is not easily struck," she acknowledged, her voice tinged with a hint of wistfulness. "For the desire to connect, to be seen and understood, is a powerful force, one that can often overshadow our need for self-preservation."

She thought back to the social gathering where she had withdrawn, her fear of vulnerability keeping her from the possibility of a meaningful connection. "In that moment, I allowed my past experiences to dictate my actions, to rob me of the chance to forge a new bond, to explore the depths of that initial spark," Shirley said, her brow furrowing slightly.

Yet, as she gazed out the window she felt a renewed sense of resolve. "But I've since learned that true strength lies not in the rigid walls we build, but in the courage to open ourselves up, to take that leap of faith and trust that we have the resilience to weather any storm that may come our way."

I found that balance, that perfect harmony between self-protection and the desire to connect," she murmured, her voice soft but resolute. "And it is a lesson I carry with me, one that I strive to impart to those I guide on their own journeys of the heart."

"My dear readers, I invite you to explore the delicate balance between guarding your heart and allowing love to enter," she said, her lips curving into a gentle smile. "For it is in the moments when we muster the courage to be vulnerable that we unlock the true potential of our connections, forging bonds that can weather even the fiercest of storms."

As the afternoon sun dipped lower in the sky, casting a warm glow over the kitchen, Shirley felt a renewed sense of purpose. The lessons she had learned, the wisdom she had gained, were not just her own – they were a tapestry woven with the experiences of countless individuals, each thread a testament to the resilience of the human heart.

"Self-protection and desire," she whispered, her lips curving into a thoughtful smile. "It is a balance that we all must navigate, but one that holds the power to transform us, to lead us to the very depths of our own hearts."

As the sun dipped below the horizon, casting a warm glow over the cozy kitchen, Shirley felt a sense of anticipation and excitement for the journey that lay ahead. For in the balance between self- protection and desire, she knew, lay the key to unlocking the true power of human connection – a power that could transform lives, heal wounds, and ignite the spark of hope within even the most guarded of hearts.

Chapter 10: Cultivating Needs and Boundaries

The warm glow of the afternoon sun filtered through the sheer curtains, casting a soft light over the familiar surroundings of Ms.

Spencer's cozy writing nook. Seated at her desk, a steaming mug of Earl Grey tea cradled in her hands, she allowed her gaze to drift over the collection of well-worn journals that lay scattered before her, each one a testament to the reflections and insights that had guided her on the journey of the heart.

With a deep, steadying breath, her fingers traced the intricate patterns on the cover of her latest journal, a sense of anticipation building within her. It was here, amidst the pages filled with her own musings and the anecdotes shared by her readers, that she found the inspiration to continue her exploration of the complexities of the human experience.

Her thoughts drifted back to a time when the delicate balance between her own needs and the desire to please others had not come so easily to her. She remembered a particular incident, years ago, when she had found herself caught in the throes of a relationship that had slowly begun to erode her sense of self.

"I was so afraid of rocking the boat, of causing any disruption to the carefully constructed world we had built together," she murmured, her fingers tightening around the warm ceramic of her mug. "And so, I found myself constantly compromising, suppressing my own desires in a desperate attempt to maintain the illusion of harmony."

She recalled the growing resentment that had simmered beneath the surface, the way her heart had ached with the weight of her unspoken needs. Ms. Spencer's brow furrowed as she remembered the way she had withdrawn, her polite smiles and casual conversation masking the turmoil that threatened to consume her.

"It was as if I had slowly become a stranger to myself," she admitted, her voice tinged with a hint of regret. "The very essence of who I was had been buried beneath the layers of expectations and the constant need to please."

Ms. Spencer's gaze drifted to the photograph that sat on the corner of her desk, a candid shot of her and her ex-husband, their arms wrapped around each other, laughter etched upon their faces. The memory of his warm embrace and infectious chuckle washed over her, a bittersweet reminder of the profound connection they had shared.

"We had built our relationship on a foundation of mutual understanding and respect, where we both felt empowered to express our needs and desires without fear of judgment or rejection."

She recalled the countless conversations they had shared, the way they had navigated the complexities of their relationship with open and honest communication. "It wasn't always easy, of course," she acknowledged.

"There were times when we disagreed, when our needs seemed to clash. But we always found a way to listen, to compromise, and to honor the unique perspectives we each brought to the table."

Her thoughts then drifted to a recent workshop she had led, where the theme of self-awareness and boundary-setting had been the central focus. As she closed her eyes, the memory of that day unfolded vividly in her mind, the charged atmosphere of the room palpable even now.

"I can still feel the mix of anticipation and apprehension that filled the air as the participants gathered," she murmured, her brow furrowing slightly. "Some were eager, their eyes shining with a glimmer of hope, while others appeared guarded, their bodies tense with the weight of their own fears and insecurities."

Ms. Spencer recalled the way she had welcomed the group, her voice warm and soothing as she guided them through a series of exercises designed to help them explore the concept of personal needs and boundaries.

"I wanted to create a safe space, a sanctuary where they could feel empowered to be vulnerable, to share their stories and their struggles without fear of judgment," she explained, her fingers tracing the rim of her mug.

As the workshop progressed, she had witnessed a profound transformation in the participants, the walls of their carefully constructed defenses slowly crumbling as they confronted the truths that lay within. She remembered one particular moment, when a young woman had stood up, her voice trembling with a mix of emotion and resolve.

"'I always thought that setting boundaries meant being selfish,'" the woman had said, her gaze meeting Shirley's with a newfound clarity. "'But now I realize that it's an act of self-respect, a way of honoring my own needs and desires.'"

Ms. Spencer's lips curved into a warm smile as she recalled the woman's words, the profound impact they had had on the entire room. "In that moment, I saw the power of community, the way in which the shared vulnerability of those present could ignite a spark of understanding and empowerment," she said, her voice filled with a quiet conviction.

Ms. Spencer's thoughts turned to the challenges she had faced in communicating her own needs to her adult children. She remembered a particularly poignant conversation with her daughter, one that had been laced with a mix of tenderness and frustration.

"I had been longing for more quality time together, to simply sit and share our thoughts and experiences without the constant distractions of our busy lives," she explained, her brow furrowing slightly. "But when I tried to broach the subject, my daughter immediately became defensive, her walls going up as she insisted that she was doing the best she could."

Ms. Spencer's fingers tightened around her mug as she recalled the emotional weight of that exchange, the way her heart had ached with the desire to be truly heard and understood.

"I could see the hurt in her eyes, the fear that she was somehow falling short as a daughter," she said, her voice tinged with empathy. "And in that moment, I realized that the key to bridging the divide lay not in accusation, but in open and compassionate communication."

With a deep breath, Shirley allowed her gaze to drift to the window, where the vibrant blooms of her garden swayed gently in the breeze. "It's a lesson I've had to learn time and time again," she murmured, her voice soft but resolute. "That the act of expressing our needs, of setting healthy boundaries, is not an act of selfishness, but one of self-respect and self-care."

Her thoughts then turned to the friendships that had enriched her life, the deep connections that had provided a sense of belonging and understanding. She remembered a particular situation where a close friend had repeatedly leaned on her for emotional support, often at the expense of her own well-being.

"I found myself constantly drained, my own needs and desires pushed to the wayside as I tried to be the rock that my friend could cling to," she recalled, her brow furrowing with a hint of frustration. "And it wasn't until I finally mustered the courage to have an honest conversation with her that I realized the true imbalance in our relationship."

She described the candid exchange that had followed, the way she had carefully articulated her feelings and the boundaries she needed to establish in order to maintain her own emotional well- being. "It was uncomfortable, to be sure," she admitted, "but the relief I felt afterwards was palpable. I finally had the courage to assert my own needs, to create a dynamic that was built on mutual respect and understanding."

As she sat in the tranquility of her writing nook, the warmth of the afternoon sun caressing her face, she couldn't help but draw a parallel between the delicate balance of her relationships and the nurturing of her beloved plants.

"Tending to our personal needs and boundaries is not unlike the care we provide for our plants," she mused, her gaze drifting to the vibrant blooms that thrived in her living room. "We must be mindful of the unique requirements of each plant, providing the right amount of water, sunlight, and nutrients to ensure their healthy growth."

She paused, a thoughtful expression crossing her features. "And just as we must be vigilant in caring for our plants, so too must we be diligent in setting boundaries that protect the integrity of our relationships and our own well-being."

"The journey of cultivating our needs and boundaries is not an easy one, my dear readers," she acknowledged, her voice warm and inviting. "But it is a necessary step in the pursuit of truly meaningful and fulfilling connections."

Embrace the courage to speak your truth, to honor your unique needs, and to build relationships that nurture and empower you.

The lessons Ms. Spencer had learned, the wisdom she had gained, were not just her own – they were a tapestry woven with the experiences of countless individuals, each thread a testament to the resilience of the human spirit. "Cultivating your needs and boundaries will shape the very essence of your lives."

Chapter 11: Emotional and Personal Autonomy

The soft autumn breeze rustled the vibrant leaves outside Shirley Spencer's cozy living room, casting a warm glow over the familiar surroundings. Nestled in her favorite armchair, a soft blanket draped over her lap, Shirley gazed out the window, her fingers tracing the delicate patterns of the quilt as she allowed her mind to drift back to a time when the pursuit of emotional and personal autonomy had not come so easily to her.

Ms. Spencer could still vividly recall the family gathering, years ago, where she had felt the weight of expectation pressing down upon her. The air had been thick with the chatter of her relatives, their voices mingling together in a cacophony of well-meaning but overbearing comments and unsolicited advice.

Ms. Spencer had forced a polite smile, she struggled to find the words to express her true desires to her mother, I've been thinking about pursuing a degree in counseling," she had replied, her voice tinged with a hint of hesitation.

The room had fallen silent, all eyes turning to her as her relatives exchanged puzzled glances. "Counseling?" But you've always been so good at numbers, at managing the finances. Isn't that where your true passion lies?"

Ms. Spencer had felt her heart racing, the weight of their expectations bearing down upon her. "It's just... something I've been considering," she had murmured, her gaze drifting to the floor as she fought the urge to shrink back into the safety of their preconceived notions.

In that moment, she had been acutely aware of the internal conflict raging within her – the desire to honor her own aspirations and the fear of disappointing the very people she loved the most. It was a struggle she had grappled with time and time again, the constant need to balance her own identity with the expectations of her family.

As Ms. Spencer sat in the warmth of her living room, the memory of that family gathering still etched in her mind, she couldn't help but reflect on the lessons she had learned in the years that followed. It was her work as a counselor, guiding individuals through the complexities of self-discovery, that had truly opened her eyes to the importance of emotional and personal autonomy.

She recalled a particularly impactful group she had led, where the theme of self-identity and boundary-setting had been the central focus. The room had been charged with a palpable energy as the participants gathered, some eager and hopeful, while others appeared guarded, their bodies tense with the weight of their own fears and insecurities.

"I wanted to create a safe space, a sanctuary where they could feel empowered to be vulnerable, to share their stories and their struggles without fear of judgment," she murmured. It was experiences like these that had reinforced her belief in the transformative power of personal autonomy. She had witnessed firsthand the way in which individuals had blossomed, their sense of self-worth and confidence soaring as they learned to prioritize their own needs and boundaries.

Chapter 12 - Navigating the Nature of Human Connection

As the warm afternoon sunlight filtered through the living room window, casting a soft glow on the pages of her leather-bound journal, Ms. Spencer found herself reflecting on the intricate nature of human connection. With a pensive expression, she traced the lines of her latest entry, the words flowing from her pen like a gentle stream.

Nestled in her favorite armchair, Ms. Spencer allowed her mind to wander back to a time when she had felt profoundly alone, despite being surrounded by loved ones. It had been during a bustling family gathering, a moment that should have been filled with laughter and camaraderie. Yet, as she observed the animated conversations unfolding around her, she couldn't help but feel a sense of disconnect, as if an invisible barrier had been erected between herself and the people she cared about.

"It's curious, isn't it?" she mused aloud, her voice warm and contemplative. "How we can be in the midst of a crowd, yet still feel utterly alone. As if our hearts are longing for a deeper understanding, a true connection that transcends the mere physical proximity."

Ms. Spencer paused, her gaze drifting to the window, where a pair of sparrows flitted among the branches of a nearby tree. "That moment taught me the importance of seeking not just companionship, but genuine, meaningful relationships – the kind that nourish the soul and bridge the gap between individuals."

Turning back to her journal, she began to write with renewed purpose, her words flowing like a river of wisdom. "Empathy, my dear readers, is the key that unlocks the door to deeper human connection. It is the ability to truly understand and share the feelings of another, to walk in their shoes and see the world through their eyes."

Ms. Spencer's mind drifted to a particularly poignant session from her years as a mental health counselor, a memory that had left an indelible mark on her understanding of the power of empathy.

"I'll never forget the day when a client, struggling to connect with their family, came to me in a state of despair," she recounted, her eyes softening with compassion. "They felt misunderstood, their cries for help falling on deaf ears. But through active listening and a genuine effort to empathize, we were able to uncover the root of the disconnect and find a path forward."

As Ms. Spencer described the transformation that unfolded, her voice took on a reverent tone. "It was as if a veil had been lifted, and the client's family members finally saw them for who they truly were. Barriers crumbled, and understanding blossomed, all because we took the time to listen, to truly hear and feel the emotions that lay beneath the surface."

She paused, a small smile tugging at the corners of her lips. "Empathy, my friends, is the bridge that connects us, the balm that soothes the wounds of misunderstanding. It is a skill that must be cultivated, for in doing so, we unlock the door to richer, more fulfilling relationships."

The memory of that counseling session lingered, and Ms. Spencer found herself reflecting on her own journey of learning to be more empathetic. "There was a time when I, too, struggled to truly understand the perspectives of others," she admitted. "But as I grew, both personally and professionally, I came to realize that empathy is not just a skill – it is a way of being, a lens through which we can view the world with greater compassion and insight."

Closing her journal, Ms. Spencer rose from her chair and made her way to the kitchen, where she began to prepare a light snack. As she moved through the familiar motions, her mind drifted to a recent community volunteering event she had attended, a moment that had further reinforced the power of human connection.

"The air was alive with the sounds of laughter and shared stories," she recalled, her eyes sparkling with warmth. "Strangers united by a common cause, working side by side, discovering unexpected common ground." She paused, a wistful smile spreading across her face. "It was during that event that I met a fellow volunteer, we found ourselves exchanging tales of our shared passion for horticulture."

Ms. Spencer's gaze grew distant, as if she could still feel the camaraderie of that moment. "In that instant, we were no longer strangers, but kindred spirits, our bond forged through the simple act of working towards a shared goal. It was a reminder that connection often arises from shared experiences and open hearts."

Returning to the present, Ms. Spencer began to assemble a tray of tea and biscuits, her movements unhurried and deliberate. "Engaging in altruistic acts can be a powerful catalyst for building meaningful relationships," she mused. "When we come together in service of others, we open ourselves up to the possibility of discovering unexpected connections – connections that can enrich our lives in profound ways.

" Ms. Spencer's thoughts turned to the importance of understanding and acceptance in relationships. Settling back into her armchair, she took a sip of her Earl Grey tea, savoring the familiar warmth and aroma.

"There was a time when a close friendship of mine faced challenges due to differing viewpoints," she recalled, her brow furrowing slightly. "We found ourselves in a heated discussion, our opinions clashing like waves against the shore. But instead of allowing the disagreement to drive us apart, we chose to listen and learn from one another."

Ms. Spencer paused, her eyes shining with a newfound understanding. "It was in that moment of openness and acceptance that our friendship deepened. We realized that embracing diversity of thought and perspective was not a weakness, but a strength – a testament to the beauty that can emerge when we approach one another with empathy and understanding."

"Nurturing connections, much like tending to a garden, requires patience, care, and a willingness to embrace the natural ebb and flow of life." "Just as each plant has its own unique needs, so too do the individuals in our lives. It is our responsibility to approach these relationships with the same level of attentiveness and respect."

With a deep breath, Ms. Spencer turned her gaze skyward, basking in the warmth of the afternoon sun. "My journey has taught me the invaluable nature of human connection – the way it can nourish the soul, challenge our perspectives, and ultimately, help us grow into our truest selves."

Closing her eyes, she allowed a sense of gratitude to wash over her. "I am grateful for the empathy, understanding, and acceptance that have enriched my relationships, both personal and professional. And I invite you, my dear readers, to embrace the beauty of human interaction, to cultivate the connections that will enrich your own lives in ways you cannot yet imagine."

"For in the end, it is the bonds we forge, the understanding we share, and the love we give that truly make us human."

Chapter 13: A Deeper Appreciation for the Human Experience

With a deep, steadying breath, Ms. Spencer opened the journal and began to pen her thoughts. "A deeper appreciation for the human experience," she mused aloud."

Ms. Spencer's eyes sparkled with a hint of wisdom earned through years of weathering life's storms. "So often, we become caught up in the whirlwind of our own lives, forgetting to pause and truly listen to the experiences of others. Yet, it is in these moments of vulnerability and connection that we discover the profound resilience and beauty that define the human spirit."

She paused, "when we open ourselves to the tapestry of emotions, thoughts, and experiences that shape the lives around us, we transcend the boundaries of our own perspectives. We find ourselves humbled by the strength of those who have weathered unimaginable challenges and inspired by the unwavering hope that shines through even the darkest of times."

Ms. Spencer's thoughts drifted to the individuals she had encountered over the years – each one a unique tapestry of experiences, triumphs, and heartbreaks. She recalled the tears of joy and sorrow that had been shed in her presence, the moments of

profound insight that had emerged from the depths of despair. It was these stories, these shared moments of the human condition, that had become the foundation of her life's work.

As a professional counselor before retirement and now a life coach, I have had the privilege of bearing witness to the transformative power of the human spirit, "she mused, her fingers tracing the edges of the journal once more. "Time and time again, I have seen individuals rise from the ashes of their own adversity, finding the strength to confront their fears and embrace the unknown with open arms."

"It is this resilience, this unwavering determination to overcome, that has become the guiding light in my own journey. For in the darkest of moments, when the weight of the world seemed to bear down upon me, it was the stories of others – their triumphs, their lessons, their courage – that inspired me to keep moving forward."

With a renewed sense of purpose, Ms. Spencer paused, a reflective smile gracing her features. "For the journey of the heart is never a solitary one, but rather a tapestry of interconnected stories, woven together by the threads of our common humanity. It is in the act of sharing, of listening, and of embracing our differences that we find the true beauty and wisdom that lies at the core of the human experience."

A deeper appreciation for the human experience arises when we acknowledge the intricate tapestry of emotions, thoughts, and connections that define our lives. Each individual story we encounter— filled with triumphs, struggles, joys, and sorrows—serves as a reminder of our shared humanity. In moments of vulnerability, we often discover profound wisdom and resilience that illuminate the paths others have walked. By fostering empathy and actively listening to diverse perspectives, we can transcend superficial judgments and connect with the underlying threads that bind us all.

Moreover, the richness of the human experience is often revealed in the smallest details: a child's laughter, the warmth of a friend's embrace, or the quiet reflection of solitude. These seemingly mundane moments hold immense significance, encouraging us to pause and reflect on our interconnectedness.

The journey through life is not defined by grand achievements alone, but by the everyday interactions and the love we cultivate. As we navigate the complexities of existence, embracing both the light and dark aspects of our shared reality allows us to cultivate a deeper sense of gratitude and appreciation for what it means to be human.

In this exploration, we learn to cherish the diversity of experiences, recognizing that each person carries their own unique burdens and joys.

The aftermath from the trauma of a heartbreak is the coldest raw deals of life and is one of the hardest experiences to mentally recover. The struggle to physically and mentally function daily is devasting.

Sometimes you find yourself just going through the motions of life. Then you find yourself lost, trying to find your way through life, unaware where and what your direction is.

You sudden realize that in the mist of all the confusion and daily struggle your life span is decreasing without the expected productive progress as you planned and hoped for your life.

The coldest deal in life is the desire to feel complete and whole with love. The human touch of love that was created from the beginning of time. The creation of a female was bonded from the rib of a male which empowers the two with the completeness to be bonded with the true powerfulness of love.

The true understanding of the power of love cannot be obtained until a person has gain the ability to learn the delicate passionate respect for the heart, for the heart is connected to a person's soul.

To gain the ability to understand the power of love, one must understand the devasting trauma as a result from the lack of a person's respect for the heart. One must pay the piper of life himself and experience the pain and trauma, for It is only then that the respect for heart can be acknowledged and respected.

Everyone pays the piper of life at least once in their lifetime for it is written, a person reaps what he sows and there is no way to avoid the piper. The piper of life reaps your soul in a way that your life is turned upside down, you never forget that pain and the knowledge obtained from the experience for it is one of the coldest lessons learned that will impact your life for a lifetime.

Let's talk about the aspects of paying the piper of life. The piper creeps into your life unexpectedly at a time you think your life is on the top of the world. Then all at once your world tumble down hill as a mud slide falling down a mountain out of control. The devastated pain from the fall cause unbearable pain that leaves you in tunnel of confusion, lack of energy, mental and emotionally weak.

Recovering from the impact of piper's rife becomes a forever ending struggle to bounce back into your lifestyle which will never be the same. The pain experienced from the piper's rife attacks creates the unforgettable respect for the heart. Respect for the human heart is the profound acknowledgement and significance of an individual's life.

I encourage and invite each of you to embrace the importance of recognizing the value and feelings of others. The world around us is compassionate where the perspective of others is deserving.

This understanding fosters a ompassionate society, one that celebrates individuality while also uniting us in common purpose. By honoring the depth of the human experience, we can create spaces for dialogue and healing, inspiring future generations to uphold these connections. Ultimately, a deeper appreciation for our humanity is a journey toward understanding, acceptance, and love, paving the way for a more compassionate world.

Let us embark on this reflective journey together and discover the transformative power that awaits us when we open our hearts to the richness of the human experience.

Chapter 14: Embracing the challenges of the future

Embracing the challenges of the future requires a mindset steeped in resilience and adaptability. As we confront an ever-evolving landscape shaped by rapid technological advancements, climate change, and shifting socio-economic dynamics, it becomes imperative to approach these hurdles not as obstacles, but as opportunities for growth and innovation. The ability to pivot in response to new knowledge and circumstances will be a key trait of successful individuals and organizations.

By fostering a culture of continuous learning and embracing a collaborative spirit, we can harness diverse perspectives to tackle complex problems and devise creative solutions that benefit society as a whole.

Moreover, the future's challenges compel us to rethink our values and priorities. The issues we face—ranging from environmental degradation to social inequality—call for a holistic approach that prioritizes sustainability and inclusivity. Individuals and communities must engage in dialogues that amplify marginalized voices and advocate for systemic changes that promote equity and justice. By championing these principles, we not only prepare ourselves to navigate uncertainty but also work towards a more resilient and harmonious world.

In addition, embracing future challenges invites us to cultivate a sense of hope and possibility. Rather than succumbing to fear and pessimism, we can draw inspiration from past successes where humanity has triumphed over adversity. The innovations born out of necessity, such as renewable energy technologies and telemedicine, exemplify our capacity for positive change when confronted with daunting scenarios.

As we look ahead, it is essential to remain optimistic, harnessing our collective ingenuity to envision and create a future that reflects our highest aspirations and values. By cultivating a mindset oriented towards challenge acceptance, we can turn potential threats into transformative experiences that enrich our lives and the world around us.

Chapter 15: Transition the process of Moving-On.

Transitioning the creative process of moving on is a profound journey that involves not just letting go of the past but actively embracing the future with open arms. This transformative phase begins when one acknowledges the emotional weight of past experiences—be it the end of a relationship, the loss of a job, or any significant change. Rather than clinging to what once was, this process encourages individuals to channel their energies into new possibilities. By reframing our mindset, we can turn nostalgia into inspiration, allowing memories to serve as steppingstones rather than stumbling blocks.

Embracing the future requires a courageous leap into the unknown, where creativity can flourish unfettered by the constraints of prior experiences. This phase is marked by exploration and experimentation, as we seek out fresh ideas, perspectives, and opportunities that resonate with our authentic selves.

Setting new goals and redefining our purpose can ignite passion and drive, transforming uncertainty into a canvas of potential. Engaging in practices such as journaling, art, or collaborative projects can further catalyze this creative process, fostering connections that enrich our journey toward the future.

Ultimately, moving on is not merely about forgetting the past; it is about integrating those experiences into our narrative while crafting a vibrant, hopeful future. This evolution allows us to develop resilience and adaptability, skills essential for navigating life's inevitable changes. By embracing the future with creativity and intent, we not only honor our journey but also pave the way for new adventures that can lead to growth, fulfillment, and a renewed sense of self. In this way, the act of moving on transforms into a celebration of life's possibilities, inviting us to paint our own unique masterpiece on the canvas of time.

Navigating through uncertainty can be daunting, but setting short-term goals is a strategic way to gain clarity and direction. As you stand on the threshold of a new beginning, it's essential to take stock of what you need to achieve these goals.

Assess your skills, resources, and support systems that will empower you to take those initial steps. By breaking down larger objectives into manageable tasks, you create a roadmap that not only makes the journey less overwhelming but also allows you to celebrate small victories along the way.

Looking backward offers valuable insights as well. Acknowledge what you had, reflecting on the experiences and relationships that have shaped your journey. This reflection provides a sense of closure and helps you appreciate the lessons learned, enabling you to carry forward the wisdom gained. Conversely, gazing forward invites you to envision the abundance of possibilities that lie ahead. Envisioning your desired future can reignite motivation and optimism, helping to dismantle the anxiety of the unknown.

As you move through this transitional phase, remember that uncertainty is often a precursor to growth and transformation. By setting short-term goals, you not only chart a path through the fog but also cultivate resilience and adaptability. Embrace the journey, recognizing that with every step, you are crafting a new narrative filled with opportunities and potential.

Chapter 16: Conclusion - Embracing your own Journey

Embracing your own journey in life is a powerful act of self- acceptance and resilience. Each individual's path is uniquely woven with experiences, challenges, and triumphs that shape who they are. In a world where external comparisons can easily lead to doubt and discontent, recognizing the value of one's own journey becomes essential.

It encourages a mindset that values growth over perfection and celebrates progress, no matter how small. By honoring our own stories, we can draw strength from past hardships and gain clarity on our aspirations.

This journey isn't just about the destination; it's about the lessons learned, the relationships forged, and the moments of joy that punctuate our lives.

Moreover, embracing your own journey involves letting go of unrealistic expectations and avoiding the trap of measuring success through someone else's lens. Each twist and turn in our paths offers unique insights and opportunities for learning.

Accepting our individuality fosters self-compassion and gratitude, allowing us to cherish our personal victories and acknowledge our struggles without judgment. When we view life as a series of personal milestones rather than a competition, we can cultivate a deeper appreciation for our own experiences and for those of others. Ultimately, this acceptance equips us to face future challenges with confidence and grace, creating a rich tapestry of a life lived authentically and fully.